MY LIFE PLUS INSTRUCTIONS ON HOW TO RAP & THINK CORRECTLY

DEDICATION

This book is dedicated to my nephews.

Note to Isaiah and Luke: Uncle Hank loves you. I expect nothing but the best from you, and as time goes by, I will always be there for you, no matter what happens.

Sincerely,

Henry Yucknut

TABLE OF CONTENTS

CAPTAIN STEEL INTRODUCTION

"The more you do, the less you wait." Take a look at the starting lineup of an NBA basketball team. You will see that as a whole, those five players are putting in more work than any single one person on their entire bench, and for that reason, they get the most playing time because of the effort displayed. With that being said, they don't have to wait. There is a reason that hard workers play more than others, and it's called putting your best foot forward. That's what earning precious playing time is. I look up to Malcolm James McCormick, the nice guy with a smile on his face. Yeah, that's him. Malcolm was there for me when I needed him most. I'll never forget when I sat up all night crying, practicing, rehearsing and going over one of Malcolm McCormicks's songs called "Poppy" in my basement in front of this big TV I utilized while studying. If anybody has gotten me past my problems in life, it's him. My mother thinks highly of him and my dad says he respects him because in the song "Two Matches (feat. Ab-Soul)" Martin Luther King Jr. is mentioned. As a schizophrenic, this was really helpful for me. I like to think that if I were at the "I Have a Dream" speech back then, I would not have been removed due to being a white male that is disabled. Who wouldn't be happy to know that they are more than welcome to the party?

CHAPTER 01

Welcome To The World

I was born August 27th, 2001, in Danbury, Connecticut, however I was raised in Deerfield, Illinois. My family consists of six: my buckshot CEO dad, Steve; a royal queen as a mother, Andrea (you pronounce it An-Dree-uh); my brother Jack; plus my sisters, Emily and Elizabeth. From kindergarten to 8th grade, I went to Bannockburn School in the tiny village of Bannockburn, Illinois and graduated from a class of roughly 16, then I stepped foot into Deerfield High School which, through my eyes, was a jungle compared to Bannockburn School. As a child, I could not keep my mouth shut. As a child, I was an issue. I cussed, threw away the family's stash of alcohol, even bullied my peers. At one point, I almost gave up, because I thought, *Why not just kill myself? Heck, there are enough people populating this planet. What do I matter?*

I fought instead of crying towards the moment when I came across my passion for books. According to Biogrophy.com, it said that one of my favorite musical artists, Christopher Lee Rios, was "Taking over his own education; Big Pun was an avid reader." That was big for me. I make music and I did then, but it made a difference to me when I realized I could strengthen my vocabulary by reading. It was intense to pick up a philosophy book, but I learned from the great Friedrich Nietzsche that there is no such thing as a genius. Nietzsche said, *"Genius too does nothing but learn first how to lay bricks, then how to build, and continually seek for material and continually form itself around it. Every activity of man is amazingly complicated, not only that of the genius: but none is a 'miracle.'"* In other words, whatever it is you're doing, someone taught you how to do that. Those kinds of things keep me humble. I also believe that not even a priest would believe he is a God. Because he doesn't. That is not how this world works. Little things add up to a bigger portion over time, and Nietzsche does a really good job at introducing his books correctly when it comes to understanding his words. He even has said to take breaks from time to time, which I found tremendously helpful. Donald Trump says, too, in his books, things like this will be where the going gets tricky. Being able to take a step up for yourself is crucial. But you also have to know when to stop. I find passion in discovering every little element, straw, and hair that adds up in a leader and collecting it and exploring their data for me to use even better.

CHAPTER 02

Money

I find that making money can come easy, it's finding your target and having motivation that is hard to come by. For me, it was the Rolex Day-Date wristwatch that Donald Trump wears. I wanted a Rolex so bad after I saw my favorite president wearing one that I took out a loan and sunk deep into debt. At first, I could sit there and give myself a round of applause, but that didn't last long. It was time to take affirmative action. I dug deep into my mind and thought of the most crazy ways to make money. I was not going to take no for an answer. I did end up breaking even, and I'm out of that $5,000 hole I was in. I remember looking at my laptop screen for a short while, but those few minutes felt like years. With one swift blow, I signed the dotted line and created "The Card Chief." I am proud to say that I started my own business. I started off with an inventory at first that contained a Charizard V Alternate full art along with a few other Pokemon cards that were at $15 or up. It was as if I was throwing a football to myself across a stadium. I'd sell the cards on TCGplayer.com and or eBay.com and then I'd get the money back and go to the same places I already have been and keep on going until I felt the need to stop. It was endless touchdowns, and the reward was getting myself back on my feet but with a nice watch and a business on my hands, too.

CHAPTER 03

Strategy

I'm sitting down with my father at a table right now discussing strategy. He says strategy is a plan or action developed to achieve a major goal. I think that it's extremely important to focus on one specific part of your whole plan, thinking with a piece at a time. When I played a competitive video game called Super Smash Brothers Melee on the Nintendo Gamecube, I did not know what I was getting myself into. Firstly, Miyamoto, the person who invented Nintendo, did not publicly host tournaments. Just to give you some background info, the early tournaments were played at GameStop and hosted by franchises such as Gamers World that were specifically run by individuals. So, getting the game started up as a competitive activity was done by entrepreneurial people rather than the official corporate owner who made the game itself. I made some friends. They immediately could tell I was a rookie at Melee. My melee associates taught me the ropes. I was mashing buttons, running around without any purpose or even a clue on what to do. In hindsight, I really needed a strategy. They were right. After a couple of hang outs and practice sessions,

I was handed a literal system on how to play Melee. I plugged in my brand-new Nintendo Game Console and it was insane. There was this different page that I have never seen before. These guys knew how to code. I clicked the start button, and I was on this screen with every single character attribute, component, training style, and mini games. I didn't know where to begin. All of the sudden, everything started clicking in my head. L canceling was the first element I chose to focus on. Then it was dash dancing. Next, wave dashing. I won a match eventually at a minor melee tournament. I was surprised and excited and it was very rewarding. I remember standing up, shaking my opponent's hand. I told him good game, and I think people sorta saw me as this legend. I held my remote upside down for all three matches; it was then that "invert" my gamertag actually made sense. I never thought that Gara, a person from Nartuto, would relate in my mind. When I put on my backpack and I left that day, I knew that bag had something special in it—the remote I used. That is a perfect example of sentimental value. I couldn't care less what controller you hand me. If I see a GameCube controller, I will think fondly of my melee days, and playing and joking around with my friends with a sense of my first taste of strategy.

CHAPTER 04

Music

I have been making music for a very long time. My very first record was put out when I was 15. Today I am 22 and a proud M.C. still. When I first started, I was really bad. I would use the same words, and it was awkward. In fact, I was doing so terribly that I didn't even notice the sloppiness. After I got better, then I started noticing things in the past that were awful in my tracks. If it wasn't for my want to get better, I would have never looked back and saw what horrible sounds I was dropping. I have a huge book stand that is completely filled with notebooks containing my own handwriting of lyrics from other musical artists. Now I think you could print lyrics rather than write them out by hand and say them, but that's what I did at first. I wrote Ultramagnetic MC's, Stetsasonic, Beastie Boys', and Eric B. & Rakim's words on a piece of paper. Then I would rap to their songs using a speaker to insert their thoughts, flows, and rhyming patterns into my brain. I'd say each and every line perfectly. Do that for a while and you're going to be filled with rhymes. Eventually, I'd discharge everything I harnessed onto a piece of paper. The results were magnificent, hundreds to thousands and eventually a total of over 1,000,000 plays across the internet worldwide. Of course, I got help from Fiverr, my promotion team. I'm very thankful for all the help I have gotten over the years from my consultants and promoters.

CHAPTER 05

Vision Board

The little things that helped me the most during my worst days were ideas like trying not to laugh due to trying to humble myself, it's rude for laughter to come out at certain times. I try not to smile, I know how rough it can get. Reading, to me, is important because I think it's a great way to ease your anxiety. I find passion in discovering every little element, straw and hair that adds up in a leader and collecting it and exploring their data for me to use even better. In the future, if I ever gain a role in this country, I would start by pointing out any no go's and how to be pro-American. I'd start by outlining what it truly means to be here and that starts with getting rid of all the school shooters. We are a wealthy nation. There shouldn't be a problem. I seriously ponder the idea of if civilians could play a part in the military. We could call them the patrol troopers. We could even try it remotely for those who are under specific stresses. The patrol troopers can even commute to their work from home just as a police officer would. I was also thinking we could have the military guarding our nation's schooling. Inside we have our area's sealed shut after the kids go through metal detectors and have a school army alongside our greatest star-spangled patriots. It could be so simple. All schools on the first day introduce everybody to General Patton and his apprentice's book "General Patton's Principles for Life and Leadership" by Porter B Williamson. It could be like a pamphlet for you to refer to on your journey through high school until college. We could even do a huge Army-style send off for the kids to pump them all up for the rest of the school year.

CHAPTER 06

Who I Want To Emulate

An assignment from Trinity International University

If there's anyone I want to be like when I grow up, it's my dad. They call him CEO. He's a strategic thinker and served two years in the Navy. The father I grew up with and still know today is a Polish legend. Outstanding teaching abilities, commitment to health and fitness, and dedication to religion are just a few things that resonate with me because of him.

My father, no doubt, is a winning teacher in various ways. My father taught me how to hit a baseball. He told me to watch the ball leave his hand. Next thing you know, I'm hitting home runs in the home-run contest. My father taught me the mentality of a soldier. Life isn't a vacation. I found myself in a tremendous amount of mental pain while I was trying to maintain a job. But my dad would insist that I keep one. Like a caterpillar that turns into a butterfly, I broke free from the inability to go to work and the stresses of holding on to a job became more and more easy. It's something that passes along to someone, even if it's in their genes or not. Just like the band Queen says, "from father to son, to son." What my father accomplished for himself and me is a great example of a man at work. "If I can do it, so can you." That's a technique that I learned from my father. Growing seeds of your own or looking up to a plant, whether that be an employee or a friend that you hope to have a connection with during your life is crucial. My dad resembles a hard worker and has coached many, but in particular, he led my sisters to a championship. I've never lost any faith in my father. He's the main plant that has controlled me and my seeds. If I was handed the opportunity to coach any sort of team, I'd hope that I would be emulating my father.

My mission at Trinity is to emulate my father's love for his religion. There always seems to be those days where I can't get anything done. I go to sleep frustrated with life. Of course, my dad isn't perfect and also has challenging days. But somehow, he always seems to push through those challenges and continue to move forward. I think everything that he's doing is helping in the name of his Lord and Savior. In conclusion, I am very grateful for the support of my father and everything he has given to me in his life.

CHAPTER 07

Transitions that Lead to Growth

Change comes from within and with the help of others. It's a balance. Times of transition can be disproportionately impactful. I have learned personally from many transition periods in my life. It started as early as when I was five and my family moved to Illinois. It continued through my school-age years. And I am still evolving today in a positive, productive way.

Leaving the only home I ever had at the age of five was both scary and exciting. When I was five years old, my family moved from Danbury, Connecticut to Deerfield, Illinois. I was nervous about leaving behind everything I knew and all my friends. When I arrived at our new house, I looked out the window and saw kids playing, and it looked like a lot of fun. My brother and I proceeded to walk the neighborhood and introduce ourselves. While I was nervous about meeting new people, I knew I had to jump in. By embracing change and being ourselves, we invited new experiences and evolved as people through the friends we made. Never doubt yourself, because in the end, you can't get anywhere without saying hello.

I played football from sixth grade to tenth grade. When eleventh grade started, I decided I didn't want to play anymore. I was very nervous about walking onto the field and telling my coach that I wasn't going to play this upcoming season. I was concerned that my teammates would be upset with me. But I had to go with my heart, be brave and tell it like it was. My coach took it well and I can still remember his parting words, "There is a switch in you. You just have to find it."

In the middle of my junior year of high school, my advisor and counselor, and I had a heart-to-heart conversation. She had possibly the sharpest eye and was very protective. She was like a mother bird to her baby chicks. I think she had a good idea what I wanted to talk to her about. I had to tell her that I was done with Deerfield High School and was going to transfer to Fusion Academy. She told me she understood and agreed that Deerfield wasn't a good fit and she was going to make the transition as smooth as possible. I walked into her office very anxious and walked out of her office feeling calmer. And we were both right because Fusion was the best thing for me. I was very fortunate to get a teacher at Fusion who became my mentor. He's not your ordinary teacher. With a knife tattooed on his neck, he was quite unique. But he was not to be judged by his looks. He got my head straight. He was there when I needed him. In fact, he was just the person I needed at that time in my life.

Same could be said for my chance meeting with that unique Doctor at Trinity International University, which was very inspiring for me. I was in my freshman year and The Doctor was my professor in "One Mission,

Many Stories." The class was required for all Trinity students and was about the role of religion in life. At the time, I didn't know what I wanted to be. I was enrolled in one of the religious disciplines. I don't know for sure if he was catholic or not, but he believed in God, our Lord and Savior, just as Jesus did. But the fact is, he showed me that you can believe in God and still be yourself. It's a spiritual battle. You don't have to commit everything to those around you. You don't have to mimic them. Do what's right for you and is in your heart. Be a lion and understand that everyone has their own roar. "But if you suffer as a Christian, do not be ashamed, but glorify God that you bear that name" (Peter 4:16). The Doctor gave me the confidence to follow my heart and pursue a career that excited me. And that career has turned out to be a business. Puzzles come together piece by piece and you never know who's going to help you fit the pieces together.

I have benefited from a great many experiences where I have learned from others, whether it be new friends after a move, an understanding football coach, an extremely insightful and protective school advisor, persuasive high school teacher or a compassionate college professor. Who I am now is also the result of personal change. I have reflected on experiences in my life and adjusted to become the person I am today. I'm certainly not done yet with my evolution. I intend to continue embracing a growth mindset. I believe anything you want in this life, you can get. Life is not a vacation, but you can make it one.

CHAPTER 08

My Donald Trump Speech

"From as early as I can remember, my father would say to me, the most important thing in life is to love what you're doing because that's the only way you'll be really good at it", said Donald Trump in The Art Of The Deal. I can tell you that in my life my dad allows me to pursue whatever job I choose. My rap career wasn't working out for me, so I decided to focus on school. In The Art Of Survival, by Donald Trump with Charles Leerhsen, it says "Toughness is pride, drive, commitment, and the courage to follow through on things you believe in, even when they are under attack. It is solving problems instead of letting them fester. It is being who you really are even when society wants you to be somebody else." Believe me, that's only a taste of what Trump's self-help books are like. In 1986 Trump accomplished one of his best achievements, the Wollman Rink. An ice skating rink that was built in 4 months using only a staggering 10 percent of New York's budget for the project. Let me give you a better perspective. In *The Art Of The Comeback* by Donald Trump with Kate Bohner, it is stated by Trump that "local government had been trying for seven years—and 20 million—to get that thing rebuilt. In 1986, I stepped in, and with 2 million, or 10 percent of the city's dollars, New Yorkers were gliding across the ice 4 months later." Today I will be discussing why you should read Donald Trump's self-help books using Monroe's Motivated Sequence. In a survey in Donald Trump's and Bill Zanker's book *Think Big And Kick Ass In Business and Life,* it states that you have a choice of getting any amount from $100,000 to 5 million dollars in the next 5 years. It's completely up to you. Nobody is telling you what to choose, so why would anyone choose $100,000? Yet in life, that is exactly what people do. Problem solving is a task that many of us have to go up against. In *Never Give Up,* a book by Donald Trump with Meredith McIver, it says "not to dwell so much on a problem that you've exhausted yourself before you can even entertain a solution. It just doesn't make sense. It takes brain power and energy to think positively and creatively and to see creatively and positively. Going negative is the easy way, the lazy way. Use your brainpower to focus on positives and your own mindset will help create your own luck."

Now I'm going to give you all a personal example of why you should read Trump's business and self-help books. My junior year of high school was terrible. So bad that I switched schools. Again, it seemed my mind wasn't at ease. So, I dropped out of high school my senior year. Around that point I found myself at Barnes And Noble all the time. I bought books and tried my hardest to read them. But I would fall short extremely often. Putting a book in my library of books I hadn't completely read yet was something I did a lot. In seemingly bad times, I went to Barnes And Noble for a complimentary visit. I passed by *The Art Of The Deal* by Donald Trump and it caught my attention. So, I gave it a try. Finally, I found a book I could read! After I finished *The Art Of The Deal* by Donald Trump, I started reading the rest of Donald Trump's self-help books. Thanks to Donald Trump, I went from the class clown to a student who participates to his fullest extent. While learning to think big, you need to surround yourself with big thinkers. Another great reason to start reading Donald Trump's self-help books is because they teach you how to defy the odds. A long time ago, people said that Donald Trump was finished when he was not doing so well financially. The same goes for me. Now Donald Trump is running for president, has a family that loves him and is still known as one of the best builders of all time, if not the top dog. Me? Well, I'm going to start a physical location soon, a store of my own. My expectations are high. Let's get three floors, one for the gamers and one for the trading card game players, and we will meet in the middle for directions.

CHAPTER 09

My New Testament Speech

Speech

Hi everyone, it's great to see you all. Today, I will be showcasing Peter

I'd like to start out by saying that Peter 1 is one of the most crucial parts of the Bible because it displays how we should treat one another. Peter focuses on what truly makes somebody a person. He emphasizes that the outside shell of a body is not what counts, it's the spirit inside that does. Peter says in 1 Peter 3:3 that "Your beauty should not come from outward adornment, such as elaborate hairstyles and the wearing of gold jewelry or fine clothes.

Rather, it should be that of your inner self, the unfading beauty of a gentle and quiet spirit, which is of great worth in God's sight."

Suffering is an essential part of Peter 1. We as humans all suffer. We go through the stresses of everyday life and ponder on if we should even exist. Peter wants us to not think that way. "If you suffer as a Christian do not be ashamed, but praise God that you bear that name." When Peter said that, in my opinion, what Peter is saying is "what doesn't kill you makes you stronger." You have to build up mental strength for your next big thing. Going through something rough is actually great for building mental strength. According to our textbook "What the new authors really cared about," 1 Peter was written during a time of persecution towards the Christians, so as a guide for Christians Peter wrote Peter 1. For they were about to face a great deal of stress just because they believed in Jesus.

I found this next part quite interesting. Peter commands us "to not repay evil with evil or insult with insult. On the contrary, repay evil with blessing, because to this you were called so that you may inherit a blessing." Once again, we're going back to Peter wanting us to think big. Repeatedly, he throws at us that what doesn't kill you makes you stronger. Because somebody went out of their way to harm you, you gained experience points. This is how you level up in Peter's mind. You get dragged down here and there both mentally and physically. Don't let that bother you, remember that you're only gaining more wisdom through tough experiences. I can definitely relate to that firsthand.

Peter 1 gives us answers to the Old Testament. In this article on Lifeway.com called "Sermon: Spiritual Success - 1 Peter 2," an anonymous sermon preached that it's not the size of the dog in the fight but the size of the fight in the dog. That's right on the money. "The secret of a successful Christian life is not in victories or perfection, but in the desire and determination of the believer. How did David beat Goliath? Because David believed in God. He was smaller and less vicious, but he was driven and had the determination of a believer.

Have you ever felt pressured because you are a Christian? Peter would encourage you to remember that Jesus also suffered and gave you an example to follow. Don't you think Jesus had anxiety? The man was sentenced to execution. Remember what I was saying earlier that Peter said in 1 Peter that you should "praise god that you bear that name." That was all Jesus could do. He asked his biological Father why he was forsaking him. But he did not abandon himself. Our holy nation depended on him dying on that cross. The Lord did not leave him. It was just the toughest part of Jesus's mission. Jesus didn't really have the time to goof off and laugh. So, every time you have a good laugh, remember that Jesus did what he did and died in the manner that the world witnessed so that we could have more good times and not just for a little while, for eternity. Pretty cool if you ask me.

In the grand scheme of things, the new birth has only just begun. In other words, the time of baptizing isn't going anywhere anytime soon. People are being baptized every day. I'm glad to say I'm an uncle of 2 nephews and their names are Isaiah and Luke. They are being raised in the Catholic faith and both have been baptized. I was very impressed when I found out that my 3-year-old nephew named Isaiah recites Our Father from memory every night before he goes to sleep.

Before we end things here, I'd just like to summarize what we went through just now. One, we went through Relationships and Beauty, my second point was Suffering.

I hope you enjoyed my speech. Thanks for being a great audience. Have a good day, everyone.

CHAPTER 10

Why Having A Job Is Important

When you have an occupation, you absolutely get an idea of what it's like to have resilience. The ability to last is crucial for your future developments in life. It is vital to pay your dues and be willing to be a low rank at first. Work your way up the ladder. You will obtain new and improved features. But only after some time. That's how life works. Be patient, the results are awesome. For me, having a job keeps me going in the right direction. Enough time has gone by for me to realize that down time can lead to bad decisions. You get bored. In my opinion, it's too easy to goof off during those times when you have nothing to do. I love momentum. Try putting your life on the line over something. You will gain a new surge of energy in this new activity. When Matthew, one of Jesus's disciples said in the Bible, "Just as the Son of Man did not come to be served, but to serve, and to give his life as a ransom for many." Matthew wrote that for the reader to emulate. Having a job is not only helping yourself, but the company you work for, and the customers too. The Christian way of life is going to work every day and providing for the Holy Spirit.

In all jobs, everything has a place and a purpose. Working around these conditions will help you gain organizational skills. Having a job is stressful, which puts you out of your comfort zone. Believe it or not, this is healthy. When you put yourself in safe but tough situations, you upgrade yourself. This world is your playing field. Even when you lose, you gain experience. But I wouldn't hold on to a losing mindset. Think like a winner. Never underestimate yourself. Always say the words "you got this."

Consistency is another rule you pick up when you're working. Every Friday, heck, every weekday you're consistently in the office. Going to work when you're supposed to will set you up for success. Next thing you know, you're consistently getting zero cavities, consistently coming home with handfuls of money, constantly making the dean's list. The possibilities are endless with proper consistency.

CHAPTER 11

The Mission For The Republicans!

I believe in spreading capitalism. That's so much easier said than done, but get yourself Adam Smith's *Wealth of Nations* and it will help. Once you have read the book, share it with others. It will help trust me. The United States is a great country. It combines democracy with freedom. Democracy allows entrepreneurs to flourish. I consider myself an entrepreneur and I am happy that I have the chance to run my own business. When it comes to freedom, one important freedom for me is freedom of religion. For me I put complete trust in my Jesus Christ that I believe in and read as many books as I possibly can. I also believe in staying productive. I am always doing something to make myself or things around me better. Stay strong, the force is within you, my friend. Find that special something.

Here are 5 things I recommend:

1. Vote for Trump during November in this upcoming 2024 election.

2. Less swearing, it's for the kids.

3. Praise and always think of The Father or The Son or The Holy Spirit.

4. Pledge of allegiance to the flag of the United States of America at every outing, no matter where you stand.

5. Give more thumbs up and less middle fingers at people. Look, I think sometimes that one is more specifically for me.

CHAPTER 12

The Champion of New York City

Rudolph W. Giuliani will forever be known as the champion of New York City. He was the hometown boy who grew to greatness and worked tirelessly to make a permanent, positive impact on the city he loved. He became mayor at a time when New York was at a very low period. The year was 1993 and crime was rampant. The city was dirty. It was losing its charm and its tourism. Giuliani changed all of that by implementing a methodical, step-by-step program to address the fundamental issues of crime and corruption. Giuliani also followed through on his mayoral campaign promise of reforming New York City's finances and providing for the poor and the needy. Giuliani was also mayor during one of the most historic and horrific events in the history of the United States, the terrorist attack on the Twin Towers. During the tragedy, Giuliani was a primary organizer of the first responder support effort, which has been held up as one of the most organized and selfless examples of human kindness by tapping into his deep sense of patriotism. By showing his direct support and putting in his own time it made the first responders feel appreciated. Giuliani then galvanized the city in a healing process that extended across the entire country and in some ways impacted the world.

Rudolph Giuliani was born in East Flatbush, New York, New York, on May 28th, 1944. Flatbush was at the time and still is today an Italian section of New York. Giuliani was an only child. His parents were Harold and Helen. Giuliani lived in Flatbush until the age of seven, when he and his family moved to Garden City, New York, New York. Rudy, as he became known in his early teens, went to St. Anne's catholic grade school in Garden City and then commuted back to Flatbush to attend Bishop Loughlin Memorial High School. He grew up in a lower, middle class or working class family setting. His parents were children of Italian immigrants and were rather strict. Giuliani's father was a boxer and instilled clear thinking into his son. Giuliani's favorite quote from his father was, "'Whenever you get into a jam, whenever you get into a crisis or an emergency, become the calmest person in the room and you'll be able to figure your way out of it" (Giuliani 290). Giuliani went to Manhattan College for his undergraduate degree and studied political science. He then went to New York University Law School and graduated cum laude with a Juris Doctor degree in 1968. The book *Leadership* (author: Rudolph W. Giuliani) was the primary source of all of this historical background information.

Giuliani was elected as the 107th mayor of NYC in 1994. He was elected in part because of his commitment to clean up the city and make it a safer place to live. He did this by starting at the bottom and working his way up. He did things like cleaning up graffiti on buildings and fixing broken windows. In fact, he called it the "broken windows theory" (Giuliani 47). Cracking down on jaywalkers was another example. He believed in "sweating the small stuff" (Giuliani 47). He got this idea in part from the architect Ludwig Mies van der Rohe, who said in the New York Herald Tribune in 1959 that "God is in the details" (Giuliani 46). Rudy is quoted as saying that this is "The best way to assure that your staff, and others who rely on you at such times, feel that someone is leading the way is to show that you're as focused as ever on the details" (Giuliani 48). Another of Giuliani's accomplishments was a reduction in crime. "During the 1990s, crime rates in New York City dropped dramatically, even more than in the United States as a whole. Violent crime declined by more than 56 percent in the city, compared to about 28 percent in the nation as a whole. Property crimes tumbled by about 65 percent but fell only 26 percent nationally" (Francis).

Another of Giuliani's accomplishments was improving the finances of NYC. When Giuliani took office in 1994, NYC was one of the most poorly run cities from a financial standpoint in the entire country. In fact, the budget deficit in December of 1993 was over 2 billion dollars (Roche). Simply put, the city was spending more money than it was taking in. This was in part due to a reduction in tourism which was tied to the high crime rate. This was also due to a drop in property values. The NY Times was quoted as saying that the deficit "...had grown by at least $250 million because of a significant decline in the assessed value of the city's real estate" (Myers). One of the main things Giuliani did was create private sector jobs, in part by reducing taxes that brought businesses back to the city that had left for the suburbs. Yes, the tax rate was reduced, but the number of businesses paying taxes went way up and more than made up for the cut in rate. He also made conventions a focus. In 1993, NYC had 50% fewer conventions than 5 years previously. Giuliani tackled this once again with a related tax cut. When Giuliani took over as Mayor, NYC hotels were charging 21.25% tax on rooms. He repealed 5% of the hotel tax and pulled back substantially on related sales taxes. All of these tax cuts lead to increased business. The increased business led to increased revenue. By 2002, the tax reductions put in place by Giuliani's administration totaled $6.5 billion. This was done through six consecutive years of tax reductions. It resulted in a shift from deficit to surplus. In fact, the surplus in 2002 was over 2 billion dollars (Roche).

September 11th, 2001 was perhaps the worst day in the history of the United States. The terrorist attacks on the Twin Towers in NYC captured the world's attention and made all of humanity feel vulnerable and at the mercy of villains. There was nothing but heartache and dismay. Clearly, the city, the country and even the world needed leadership. That leadership came from Rudy Giuliani. And it began the day of the attacks. Giuliani went to the site of the Twin Towers as soon as he heard the news. He did this because he was taught to "see things with your own eyes and set an example" (Giuliani, preface XIV). He then went into action. He started by setting up communications. He made sure the first responders and the people attending to the injured were organized and getting everything they needed. He then went on to be the voice of calm and resolve. He didn't let people focus on hate or pity. The focus was on the saving of as many lives as possible. Giuliani galvanized the city by giving all the credit to the first responders. He said to all "they didn't wonder whether the people in those buildings were black or white, young or old, Muslim or Christian or Jew, they simply rushed in and accomplished the greatest rescue in the history of this country" (Giuliani, preface XVI). He was equally impressive during the healing process. NYC and the entire country were living in fear after that terrible day. Giuliani stepped in and provided courage. He made it a point to personally attend as many funerals as he possibly could with the idea that funerals are mandatory and weddings are discretionary (Giuliani 253). He was awarded Time Magazine's person of the year in 2001 for his efforts. Time stated "He was the gutsy decision maker, balancing security against symbolism, overruling those who wanted to keep the city buttoned up tight, pushing key institutions — from the New York Stock Exchange to Major League Baseball — to reopen and prove that New Yorkers were getting on with life" (Pooley).

Critics of Giuliani during his term as mayor suggest he had ulterior motives and was taking advantage of the 9/11 crises to improve his own image. The biggest critics were those who said he put first responders in harm's way for his own gain. NBC news captured the emotion during a May 19th, 2004 hearing on the handling of the 9/11 attacks. Monica Gabrielle, whose husband was killed, said the panel and Giuliani spent the morning "cloaking everything in heroism." "We leave frustrated," she said. "They made a huge faux pas in letting Rudy Giuliani polish his crown" (NBC News reporter). In the more recent past Rudy Giuliani has also been criticized for his association with Donald Trump. Donald Trump has had numerous legal issues and Giuliani has been vocal about his support for Trump. This has raised concerns regarding Giuliani and his judgment.

Rudy Giuliani was a true champion of New York City. He became mayor at a time when New York was at one of its lowest points. The city was filthy dirty. The city was filled with crime. The city was losing money. Giuliani came in and changed all of that and turned it into a well-run city. He started by sweating the small stuff and created a culture of attention to details. He led by example. And he did that on the biggest stage when he led the city through the traumatic experiences inflicted by the terrorists on 9-11 by staying calm and focused. Giuliani's motivation was simple. He was a proud resident of NYC and wanted to do all he could for his city and to this day is standing up for the city he loves. He does so by never forgetting his father's words of advice to be the calmest person in the room and get the job done.

CHAPTER 13

The Whisper Keyboard

This chapter is intended to encourage creativity and entrepreneurship. I have an idea. See what you think. Keyboards are noisy. As such, they can be a distraction, not only to the user, but to people who are nearby. We have come up with a solution, the Whisper Keyboard. The Whisper Keyboard is silent. It allows the user to type in peace and quiet. It is made of durable, lightweight, non-slip natural rubber material, similar to a mouse pad. It can be rolled up and put into an easy to carry tube. It connects to the laptop via an embedded Bluetooth chip. No wires! The Whisper Keyboard comes in 6 different standard colors, or you can have it custom made with your own design or photo.

Let's face it, keyboard clicking is annoying and distracting and a standard keyboard can be uncomfortable and tiresome. Not only does the sound of a standard keyboard bother the user, but it also bothers people nearby. Why should neighbors need to hear you type? Our solution is perfect for classroom settings, libraries and even the home environment. Teachers will not have to listen to a room full of clicking and clacking. Your friends and family members will be able to watch TV in peace. People studying around you in the library can keep their focus. Students would be a key market target, but the reality is the majority of the population today uses a keyboard (note: we will conduct research to determine the number of Americans who use a keyboard or laptop). Business is also a great application. Today, many businesses have "open seating" instead of cubes or offices. The Whisper Keyboard would be perfect for these environments. The Whisper is also well suited for business centers where consumers can rent computer time. We also believe the Whisper will be therapeutic and reduce anxiety for the user.

We have conducted preliminary market research across fellow students and family members. Everyone we've spoken to likes the idea of the Whisper Keyboard. We are going to do additional, more statistically significant research via questionnaires. We are also going to conduct additional research in the workplace tapping into family and friends that work in office settings.

CHAPTER 14

Speculating Implementation Of The Whisper Keyboard

Our organizational design and growth plan is constructed from our operational plan. We are planning to start out rather lean, relying disproportionately on ourselves and a few key employees, while outsourcing some of the technically challenging jobs. We believe in our product and think the Whisper Keyboard will have a real impact on the market. What we don't know is scale and the rate at which we will scale. Forecasting demand is going to be tough at first. Therefore, we are erring on the side of caution and starting out with fewer employees, doing limited production runs and then letting scarcity in the market drive further demand. When we get a handle on the amount of demand and the relative rate of growth, we'll shift our focus to building the right size organization and better determine what should be in-house and outsourced permanently.

There are a few roles we will need on day one. The first is the Director of Operations. We need someone with a technical background who is experienced in both computer technology, manufacturing, procurement and supply chain to get this off the ground. We anticipate this person to have at least 10 years of experience in related fields, so they are going to be a bit higher salary. They will be responsible for finalizing design with a third party, sourcing materials, setting up production (internal and external) and ultimately putting together a production schedule with a demand plan. We think that person can do most of the work themselves with one support person who will be an entry level (engineer right out of college). They will also hire temporary staff to do the operational assembly of the finished product, packaging and shipping. We think two temps on a one shift basis will do it.

We will also need someone running Sales and Marketing day one. We plan to have the role be combined at the beginning. One of our team members will serve that role in the beginning. He will be a founder/CEO and head of Sales and Marketing. He will be responsible for creating a marketing campaign and figuring out how to go to market. We plan to start selling on-line to get our name out there and then expand to physical stores. When we go to physical stores, we will first start by going through a distributor. He will do all the work for the first six months and then add staff as we grow. We are planning for one person in Marketing and one person in Sales at entry level 6 months after we are in production. Both will come right out of college with the Sales person having a Bachelor's in Business and the Marketing person having an MBA.

We will also need a head of Finance day 1. There are lots of financial assumptions we will need to work through, from cost of goods sold to distribution to selling price. We do not think this will be too complicated in the beginning and therefore think a team member can fill that role in the beginning. He will be Founder/CEO and head of Finance. Under him will be a Financial Analyst. We think a person with a Bachelor's in Finance with two to three years of experience would work. They will not have additional staff for quite some time.

I will take on responsibility for Human Resources and running the office day-to-day. I will be Founder/CEO and head of HR. I will not have any additional staff at the beginning. We will need a small space that will serve as both our office and our assembly area. As we stated in our operational plan, we intend to outsource the technical work associated with Bluetooth production and keyboard sensor creation. We plan to assemble, package and ship from our small location until we get to scale. We think we need about 3000 square feet for 6 to 7 offices and an assembly area.

A big part of who we want to be culturally is associated with our Christian mindset. When we recruit and interview we will be looking for people who are hard-working and smart, but also caring. One of our company's philosophies will be "What Would Jesus do in This Situation?" We think if we can build a team that cares as much for each other and the world around them as they do about the Whisper Keyboard, we will be very successful.

CHAPTER 15

Self-Reflective Essay

Why as Christians should we care about art? Some would say that art is a distraction from religion. I disagree. I think art provides me with another way to get closer to Jesus and interpret the world around me by challenging me to think hard about what it is I'm looking at or listening to. This past semester in Art Appreciation has been very fulfilling. It's helped me reflect on my own personal experiences involving art and exposed me to thoughts and influences from many others. This paper will capture my own personal thoughts and those that came to mind when reading *Art for God's Sake: A Call to Recover the Arts* by Philip Graham Ryken and "A Strategy for Cultivating the Beautiful," a chapter in Amy Sherman's book *Agents of Flourishing: Pursuing Shalom in Every Corner of Society*

When I first came across Luke's Wall it was as part of an instrumental in a song by Black Sabbath called "War Pigs/Luke's Wall" and I immediately concluded that the lead singer and author of the song, Ozzy Osbourne, was a faithful Christian because he was incorporating a very

Christian reference into what many think of as a scary song. Luke's wall is a reference from the Bible (Luke 1:37) that states "For with God, nothing shall be impossible." It is an anti-war song. That led me to thinking about *The Red Square* by Kazimir Malevich and *Study for Homage to the Square* by Josef Albers which we studied in Art Appreciation. In class, it was the most time we spent on a single painting. My Professor had to heavily guide the class so we could appreciate the message of simplicity and better understand that when painting one doesn't have to complicate with lines, objects and images. The Black Sabbath song and the painting by Malevich are similar in that they encourage the listener/viewer to interpret in their own way. I listen to Luke's Wall, and I want to sprint toward standing up for what is good. When I see Malevich's painting, I want to take a knee or remove my hat in honor of those who have passed. The red color in Malevich's painting is a lot like the destruction that is implied in Luke's Wall.

Philip Ryken does a great job in *Art for God's Sake: A Call to Recover the Arts* explaining to the reader that God is present in art. The reference to Exodus 31 and how God directed two specific men, Bezalel and Oholiab to be the artists that would construct the tabernacle for Moses was helpful. The book calls out four specific fundamentals. "The artist's call and gift come from God." "God loves all kinds of art." "God maintains high standards for goodness, truth and beauty." "Art is for the glory of God." It was particularly helpful to be able to put scary art in proper perspective. Not all art has to be kind and soothing and pretty. Life is not always kind. Jesus was crucified in a very mean and hateful and brutal way. Capturing that pain is part of the truth that Ryken talks about. It was also helpful to see the direct connection between the choices of Bezalel and Oholiab and how they were gifted by God. Exodus states "I have filled him with skill, ability and knowledge of all kinds of crafts" when talking about Bezalel. And Exodus says that Oholiab is "a craftsman and designer, and an embroiderer in blue, purple and scarlet yarn and fine linen." Their talents came from God. This was reinforced by the quote from the composer Igor Stravinsky who said, "I take no pride in my artistic talents; they are God-given and I see absolutely no reason to become puffed up over something that one has received." The term "puffed up" hit home with me. I like modesty. I also thought it was very cool that John Sebastian Bach signed all his works with "sDg," which stood for soli-Deo-gloria, which is Latin for "to God alone be the glory." Bach didn't want to take credit. He wanted all the glory to go to God.

Amy Sherman's *book Agents of Flourishing: Pursuing Shalom in Every Corner of Society* has a great chapter called "A Strategy for Cultivating the Beautiful: Invest in the Art" where she provides the reader a wonderful story about work being done in Kansas City at the Christ Community Church. One painting that hangs in the Church is called "The Four Chapters" and it is called that because it is intended to capture creation, the fall, redemption and consummation. It is to me very similar to Ryken's fundamental point about goodness, truth and beauty. Not everything is perfect in life. There is pain and suffering, but there is also redemption. The Church is on a mission to help people through art. They focus much of their time and attention on young people to create a contagious culture. One of the Church members is Leigh Ann Dull and she has a great quote that says "To be fully flourishing in God's design, the arts and beauty must be a part of our lives." To her, it's about intellectual and spiritual curiosity. It shouldn't just be words that help Christians understand God. Pictures, paintings and songs can all play a vital role in helping folks to get a better handle on things. I also thought one of the projects the Church supported called "indispensable" was very smart. They gave homeless people in the Kansas City area digital cameras and asked them to go out into the community and take pictures for the purpose of art. It gave them purpose and it allowed others to see the world through their eyes. They also did events associated with the Underground Railroad and with Latino immigrants. One of the community members had a great quote, "Our culture has shut out many Christian messages, but it can still hear beauty." They are doing great things in Kansas City, and I hope it gets contagious.

I enjoyed my time in Art Appreciation this past semester. It opened my eyes to how art can help me get closer to God and understand Jesus better. Life is something to be lived and interpreted. Art helps provide alternate ways to make sense out of things. Paintings can challenge the viewer to gain valuable insights into life. Music can challenge the listener to find meaning behind thoughtful lyrics. I sincerely believe I am a better Christian having put genuine time and effort into making the most of my time in Art Appreciation.

CHAPTER 16

Take a Stand and Propose a Solution: Our Lord in Non-religious Activities

Present the Issue

Does Jesus Christ, our Lord, play a role in non-religious activities? This is a question that could be applied to many things. One area in particular is business. Our Lord is everywhere, whether you like it or not. However, when connecting religion with business, do God and Jesus have a place? A simple way of defining business is a series of deals. In every deal, both sides are negotiating. If there is a Christian in a negotiation when a trade takes place, you will also find God. This paper is dedicated to promoting the role of religion in business.

Perspective #1

One perspective you will find is that religion and business shouldn't be combined. To some, religion is a distraction and irrelevant to business. In fact, some would say it slows down the process. Let's use the example of real estate to express the point. Why should religion be involved when deciding how to make a good trade or a good buy or a good sell? If there's going to be a building put up in New York city in place of an old broken-down factory, why does God or Jesus have anything to do with it? Nobody will be offended, and everything will be OK if the building is constructed with no mention of God or Jesus. Business is business, not religion. It is a black and white position. There is no gray. Keep them separate.

Perspective #2

Others say you should only combine religion with business when it is relevant. For example, let's say a church is going to be built in place of a library. There's going to be some heat on the folks putting up the church. This is where religion and business have to be balanced. The person in charge of building the church is thinking of putting God first. However, people who don't value religion would say they get more personal benefit out of a library. Clearly, the two topics need to be debated, and religion can be involved. This perspective is an "it depends" perspective. Sometimes religion and business should coexist, sometimes there is no relevance.

My Perspective

My perspective is that religion and business should be combined and that our Lord can play a very important part in non-religious activities. I respect those who believe in perspective number one and say that religion and business are completely separate. I respect those who believe in perspective 2 and say that religion and business should only interact in certain circumstances. As a Christian, I take a different stance. I believe that bringing religion and our Lord into business is a very effective way of advancing belief in Christ and all that he stood for. Christ can play a role in all aspects of our lives. The buyer or seller sitting across the table from each other in business could have some position on religion. Maybe that person is a believer in the Jewish religion. Possibly that person is an atheist. People of all religious faiths and even those who don't believe should be given a fair shake. Whenever a Christian is making a deal, he has the attitude of supporting his/her Christian faith. In a perfect world, both parties in a business deal leave feeling that they have gotten a fair trade.

The US government has taken a stance. The Civil Rights Act of 1965 "prohibits businesses from discriminating against employees based on the basis of religion." That's a good foundational first step. I am here at Trinity International University for a reason and that is to get closer to God with the help of my professors and the classes I take. Incorporating religion with business in my opinion is a great way of doing that. Clovis G. Chappell, a highly regarded author from the 1950s, said, "A religion that does not permeate and purify and uplift and sanctify business and business relations is not the religion of Jesus Christ." As Christians, we should take every opportunity to move the world closer to God and to Jesus Christ and that includes business. I am taking a business class next semester here at Trinity and I'm excited to hear what they have to say.

Conclusion

Should religion be a part of business? Certainly, you know what I think. Business has a big impact on the way people in this world behave and I think it's the perfect place to bring Jesus Christ into the conversation. But the rest is really up to you to decide. I hope that my paper has helped you formulate an opinion on this.

CHAPTER 17

Poetry of Henry Yucknut

Where I'm From

As I walk outside, with the leash in my hand.

I wanted my neighbor to run, why couldn't he stand?

A scar that's never going to go away.

Oh why oh why did I do it on that day.

Pucks going faster than cheetahs playing tag.

I live to see the American Flag.

It is raised near the houses to the north and the west.

It's just what I need before going to rest.

Jessie and James, the TV always plays.

I wore Ash's hat, that was definitely a phase.

Video games inside of homes.

Papa looks up to Sherlock Holmes.

Instant coffee before heading to hockey.

I tried my hardest not to be too talky.

A Christian I am, it's what I discovered.

Watches on my wrist, clothes folded by my mother.

Just like some others, I went to church.

And as we sang, we threw out the devil's curse.

Leave it alone, Grandpa said.

That we did and threw our ideas off the ledge.

Ding dong ditching and trick or treating.

Halloween costumes and amino energy.

The sun always rises in the east.

I wake to find my mind at ease.

Concentration, find the cards.

Using my brain is very hard.

Listening to Dad crunch on his fruit.

After eating a goldfish, he cracked open his tooth.

Cats crying, sounding like babies.

They're happy because they just ate some crunchies.

Jack's bass booming through the walls,

so loud it sounds like a waterfall.

Dad is using the snowblower on the driveway.

Wow, the neighbors can even hear it that far away.

I smell the coffee brewing, I drink a cup then keep going.

CHAPTER 18

Transition Moments In My Life

I have struggled in my life with depression. Too many have pushed me past all of my danger. But one day we can repay them. It takes a lot to change. I believe that philosophy is crucial to solving the most severe problems. From the ancient Greeks to the German idealists, their ideas are extremely helpful. I would like to learn, maintain, and spread the great perennial thoughts. I had many would say that change is an act that switches you into somebody else. But the difference on this planet I have come across many times is the act of being like my grandfather, the World War 2 veteran. Beyond my comfort zone, I took on a journey into the digital world as a Marine would do. With every job I took, every song I published on the web, I took it to heart as a soldier. Finding common ground and bridging the generational gap is something we all need to accomplish. Personally, I tried to connect with my grandfather by thinking and reading what he went through. My dad told me to read *General Patton's Principles for Life and Leadership,* so I did. I started finding out some other things too, in fact this quote by Winston Churchill gave me goosebumps: "Never give in, never give in, never give in!" He screamed it at his British Army before defeating Germany; one of the reasons Churchill won was because of his public speaking. The outcome of Britain's battle swerved towards England in their victory is sheer devotion on Churchill to the service of one's country.

Moving to Illinois was the journey I needed because I had to get past a tough battle with my family. I got much intelligence from that scenario I was in, and it made me feel comfortable yet strong like Churchill. Upon moving into our new house, it was apparent that there were many other kids within my age range in the neighborhood. Just by looking outside of my window, I would see kids playing and it looked like a lot of fun. While I was nervous to meet new people, something in me still had the courage inside to introduce myself. This taught me a valuable lesson I brought with me throughout my life to "never doubt myself" because at the end of the day you can't get anywhere without saying hello.

One of the people who I met that helped me get to where I am today, was a friend of mine named Dylan. Dylan showed me the fun and excitement in the world of football. When I was in 4th grade, I decided to join the local peewee football team. I continued to play until my junior year of high school. But the excitement that I had from playing in fourth grade turned into a desire to never play again. This idea came to fruition, and I decided to quit playing. Unfortunately, this habit of giving up when the going got tough carried into my academic life. Within that same junior year of high school, I had begun struggling immensely within my studies. My motivation to continue striving toward success had been seemingly eliminated knowing that I could always just drop out similarly to the way I stopped playing football. This was the straw that broke the camel's back. My life began to fall apart at the seams, and it became clear that I needed some structure. I learned that you cannot quit and expect to still do well. I re-enrolled back into school before it was too late, and I graduated with a high school diploma. Everything was not always so stressful during these times.

Every year I went on a vacation with my family, or sometimes with my mom's extended family, as a family reunion. When I'm just with my family, it's easy going. For example, we love roller coasters. We would go to Disney World in Florida and camp out at Islands of Adventure in order to be the first ones in the park. When I'm on vacation for a family reunion, there are at least 17 of us and it can be hectic. Dinners are crazy. My Grandpa loves to have a good time. One time we went to a Greek restaurant with belly dancers and my ninety-four-year-old grandfather got up and danced. Talent is everywhere. I see that my nephew didn't know what was going on in that scenario. He is four years old. The Greek philosopher Socrates said, "But all I know is that I know nothing." In my mind, my nephew who was four years old was wondering what was going on. But I guess from Isaiah's perspective, if my grandpa likes it, then sure, I'll give it a try, and he got up and danced too. With that being said, I can look into this world through different lenses because of this time spent with my extended family.

Speaking of my extended family, I have only received positive feedback in regards to pursuing a higher education. From the beginning, I wanted to go to Trinity. I wanted to live close to home and everything was working out great until the school decided to go 100% virtual. During the three semesters I was there, I enjoyed the Old Testament class, the New

Testament class, and all of the public speaking I had to do. But since Trinity has now gone virtual, I am now here at CLC and their hospitality has more than impressed me. This is my second semester, and I am really enjoying English and also Marketing. My goals at CLC are to finish my associate's degree in business and then possibly transfer to Lake Forest college to pursue a degree in business. I am feeling very fortunate that my education is leading me towards a greater goal, to get my bachelor's degree in business.

The bottom line is that we all need to look up to our elders and even give the younger folks a chance. I think we need to treat America as a nation that is ruthlessly respectful to others. It's okay to have therapy sometimes. I struggle with mental problems, but I talk to someone when I'm feeling down and it really does help to see your thoughts from a different perspective. This is all so important to me because we need to get rid of this stigma that is this baloney of all stressors, that going to therapy makes you look bad. It should not be that way.

CHAPTER 19

Hero Stories! Ancient Vs. Modern

Hero Stories!

Ancient Vs. Modern

<u>Main Idea</u>: People have told stories about heroes since the beginning of human history.

Questions:

1. How are ancient hero stories similar to modern ones?

    - In all times there have been heroes of all kinds: good, evil, in between

    Good: Jason, Perseus, Hercules → Superman

    Evil: Calibos

    In Between: Hades, Odysseus → Batman

    -   Ancient heroes and modern heroes use special equipment and tools to do their heroic shiz, and they have special powers that define who they are.

Through all times and places in human civilization, people have told stories about heroes. Today, stories about heroes are just as popular as they were in ancient society, and there is plenty of evidence to show how old stories about heroes have influenced the new ones.

Then, you need to tell people HOW you're going to explain these two things (why do people like hero stories and what is their history).

When diving into a modern hero story you will find there're many characters and lights that differentiate between point of views in life. Not that one is worse than another, but that they personally go out of the way to place themselves in a setting they prefer.

Hercules vs Superman.

Hercules is strong, not entirely human. Learned from his partners. Has a pet Pegasus.

Superman is very similar, and he learns from his parents.

How are they different? One of the main differences between ancient and modern heroes is that ancient heroes were respected highly for their great achievements, even if they did do it for their own desires. Modern heroes need to have a sense of morality for they work for the people. Even though there are a lot of similarities there are also differences. Ancient heroes tried to achieve fame and glory. Modern-day heroes accomplish great deeds to satisfy the public. Lastly, the look on a hero can distinguish what era they are from. Ancient heroes look more like cavemen or any average person from ancient times. Modern day heroes are straight out of a cereal box. They are kid friendly mascots that try to gain your attention by wearing crazy fun colors. Another good example of a similarity between ancient and modern heroes is that they both have special equipment, tools, and weapons that give them heroic skills and powers. From an alien-like otherworldly blaster to an enchanted helmet from the gods.

1. Hercules - good. Superman - good. Odysseus - between. Batman - between.

2. This is also true about old stories. A lot of people might think that ancient heroes are much simpler than modern heroes, but really there are also many kinds of heroes with different points of views. It doesn't make a difference if this is true in both realms.

CHAPTER 20

From Odysseus to Batman: The Evolution of Hero Stories

Through all times and places in human civilization, people have told stories about heroes. Today, stories about heroes are just as popular as they were in ancient society, and there is plenty of evidence to show how old stories about heroes have influenced the new ones. When diving into a modern hero story, you will find there're many characters and lights that differentiate between point of views in life. Not that one is worse than another, but that they personally go out of the way to place themselves in a setting they prefer. This is also true about old stories. A lot of people might think that ancient heroes are much simpler than modern heroes, but really there are also many kinds of heroes with different points of views. It doesn't make a difference if this is true in both realms. Another good example of a similarity between ancient and modern heroes is that they both have special equipment, tools, and weapons that give them heroic skills and powers, from an alien-like otherworldly blaster to an enchanted helmet from the gods.

Even though there are a lot of similarities, there are also differences. One of the main differences between ancient and modern heroes is that ancient heroes were respected highly for their great achievements, even if they did do it for their own desires. Ancient heroes tried to achieve fame and glory. Modern day heroes accomplish great deeds to satisfy the public. Lastly, the look on a hero can distinguish what era they are from. Modern day heroes are straight out of a cereal box.

Superman is a character that supports the good side only. Superman is always defending the people that represent good in every scenario. Superman went for decades without losing a fight. An ancient version of superman is Hercules.

There are also more characters that exist in between good and evil. In ancient hero stories Odysseus is a good example. In modern hero stories though Batman is like Odysseus. Both characters are highly intelligent and use their brain power to win all of their battles. Batman is a technology wiz and creates the tools he needs to win. He's known for his batmobile and insane gadgets that he and his professors create to take on the world. Odysseus is the same way, he made the trojan horse using his craft skills. Inside there were many men and they blew out and caused mayhem. They won an entire war that they have been fighting for 10 straight years.

Finally, we have our characters that are closer to the evil side of the spectrum. All though they can be seen as straight up lunatics, there is very well a reason for their work. With so much corruption in the world it can be hard to see behind the scenes who's pulling the strings. With people like Superman, it can make it extremely difficult for dark looking forces to do their work, so they get treated very poorly due to misguided minds.

Deadpool is a great anti-hero from the modern times who is not allowed to join any hero teams, so he has to become a mercenary. While he's considered a villain we see that he's capable of doing good things. In a conflict, the X-Men come to Deadpool and ask for his help to rescue someone from the team and he saves the day.

The "Olympians" comic series by George O'Connor shows that ancient hero stories can still be entertaining to modern readers, and the way that they do that is by looking like modern comic books. This shows the connection between these old and new hero stories in an interesting way. With so many fairy-like colors and shiny objects, the readers' eyes are glued to the page, the dialogue is super goofy and fun to read, and the original stories are simplified so they're easy to read. Hera's book is the most entertaining if you ask me. There's an abundance of jokes with all the cheating between Hera and Zeus. It shows that even the top gods are not 100% good. Heracles makes his debut and the reader gets a different taste from the normal setting of the ancient story. Part of the story takes place in a verdant rainforest. If you want a better understanding of the connection between old and new stories, this series is a great place to start.

CHAPTER 21

Epilogue

Whatever you grow up to be—a politician, a businessman, an author, or a musician—make sure your occupation is loved by yourself. No matter where you are, please try. "It's not the size of the dog in the fight, it's the size of the fight in the dog." Put a chip on your shoulders. When I played hockey, my coaches always instilled in us that the game is not over until the third period is. Before we even got on the ice we had a full head of steam and it would feel like we were losing. Having that element of surprise can be deadly. Nobody will see it coming if you're pretending like you're finished. Fight as if your life's on the line every time in every outing. One of my football coaches lost his sister due to cancer. When my coach went in for surgery after the passing the doctors requested he take off his cancer support wristband. He refused. With one hard shot the IV went through his wristband and into his bloodstream. I tell this story because you have to defy the odds. My coach wasn't planning on saying yes to taking off his wristband. He knows and sees how bad this planet can be. But he went against the doctor's orders, still got the job done and has a story to tell about his sister. Now you need to be the one working, hustling and not struggling. Get out there and make something happen. Ladies and gentlemen, let's have a get signed kind of attitude! Henry wants you to work hard, be smart, and make good decisions and that starts with staying out of trouble. Let's try to remember that we are all one here in America, we all are welcome here in America, and together we will all Make America Great Again!